THE ULTIMATE CHRISTMAS MATHS BOOK FOR KIDS 6-10

THIS BOOK BELONGS TO

____

SCAN THE QR CODE BELOW TO CHECK OUT OUR OTHER BOOKS

BOOK CONTENTS

USE THIS PAGE TO SHOW YOUR WORKINGS OUT

OR IF YOU DON'T NEED TO WRITE DOWN YOUR WORKINGS OUT FOR THIS ACTIVITY, USE THIS PAGE TO DRAW SOMETHING CHRISTMAS RELATED LIKE A CHRISTMAS PRESENT OR FATHER CHRISTMAS

CHRISTMAS SUMS #1

— ADDITION —

 = 2  = 1

ANSWERS ON PAGE 51

+ = ___

+ + 4 = ___

+ 2 + 3 = ___

+ + = ___

+ 2 + = ___

USE THIS PAGE TO SHOW YOUR WORKINGS OUT

OR IF YOU DON'T NEED TO WRITE DOWN YOUR WORKINGS OUT FOR THIS ACTIVITY, USE THIS PAGE TO DRAW SOMETHING CHRISTMAS RELATED LIKE A CHRISTMAS PRESENT OR FATHER CHRISTMAS

HOW MANY ELVES? #1

THE CHRISTMAS LIST BELOW SHOWS HOW MANY ELVES ARE NEEDED TO MAKE EACH PRESENT. CAN YOU WORK OUT HOW MANY ELVES WOULD BE NEEDED FOR THE ENTIRE LIST?

ANSWER ON PAGE 53

CHRISTMAS LIST

PRESENT:	ELVES NEEDED:
BOX OF CHOCOLATES	2
BOARD GAME	3
COMPUTER GAME	1
NEW SHOES	4
COLOURING BOOK	2

TOTAL NUMBER OF ELVES NEEDED: 

USE THIS PAGE TO SHOW YOUR WORKINGS OUT

OR IF YOU DON'T NEED TO WRITE DOWN YOUR WORKINGS OUT FOR THIS ACTIVITY, USE THIS PAGE TO DRAW SOMETHING CHRISTMAS RELATED LIKE A CHRISTMAS PRESENT OR FATHER CHRISTMAS

CHRISTMAS SEQUENCES #1

CAN YOU FINISH THESE MATHS SEQUENCES AND WORK OUT WHICH NUMBERS SHOULD BE IN PLACE OF THE PRESENTS?

SEQUENCE 1:	2	5	8	11	14		
SEQUENCE 2:	1	3	5	7	9		
SEQUENCE 3:	3	6	9	12	15		
SEQUENCE 4:	2	6	10	14	18		
SEQUENCE 5:	3	8	13	18	23		

ANSWERS ON PAGE 57

USE THIS PAGE TO SHOW YOUR WORKINGS OUT

OR IF YOU DON'T NEED TO WRITE DOWN YOUR WORKINGS OUT FOR THIS ACTIVITY, USE THIS PAGE TO DRAW SOMETHING CHRISTMAS RELATED LIKE A CHRISTMAS PRESENT OR FATHER CHRISTMAS

CHRISTMAS EQUATIONS #1

CAN YOU WORK OUT HOW MUCH THE DECORATION, SNOWFLAKE AND CHRISTMAS TREE ARE WORTH?

ANSWER ON PAGE 59

 +  = 3

 +  = 7

 +  = 7

 = 3

 = 2

 = 1

USE THIS PAGE TO SHOW YOUR WORKINGS OUT

OR IF YOU DON'T NEED TO WRITE DOWN YOUR WORKINGS OUT FOR THIS ACTIVITY, USE THIS PAGE TO DRAW SOMETHING CHRISTMAS RELATED LIKE A CHRISTMAS PRESENT OR FATHER CHRISTMAS

12 DAYS OF CHRISTMAS #1

— ADDITION —

CAN YOU COMPLETE THESE MATHS QUESTIONS BASED AROUND THE 12 DAYS OF CHRISTMAS SONG?

A)	THE NUMBER OF FRENCH HENS	+	THE NUMBER OF GOLD RINGS	=
B)	THE NUMBER OF MAIDS-A-MILKING	+	THE NUMBER OF PIPERS PIPING	=
C)	THE NUMBER OF DRUMMERS DRUMMING	+	THE NUMBER OF LADIES DANCING	=

ANSWER ON PAGE 61

1 PARTRIDGE IN A PEAR TREE	5 GOLD RINGS	9 LADIES DANCING
2 TURTLE DOVES	6 GEESE-A-LAYING	10 LORDS-A-LEAPING
3 FRENCH HENS	7 SWANS-A-SWIMMING	11 PIPERS PIPING
4 CALLING BIRDS	8 MAIDS-A-MILKING	12 DRUMMERS DRUMMING

THE ULTIMATE CHRISTMAS MATHS BOOK FOR KIDS 6-10

GREAT WORK!!

YOU'VE DONE SOME GREAT WORK SO FAR SO IT'S TIME TO TREAT YOURSELF TO A FUN ACTIVITY! COLOUR IN THE IMAGE BELOW TO BRING IT TO LIFE.

USE THIS PAGE TO SHOW YOUR WORKINGS OUT

OR IF YOU DON'T NEED TO WRITE DOWN YOUR WORKINGS OUT FOR THIS ACTIVITY, USE THIS PAGE TO DRAW SOMETHING CHRISTMAS RELATED LIKE A CHRISTMAS PRESENT OR FATHER CHRISTMAS

CHRISTMAS SUMS #2

— SUBTRACTION —

 = 2  = 3  = 1

ANSWERS ON PAGE 63

 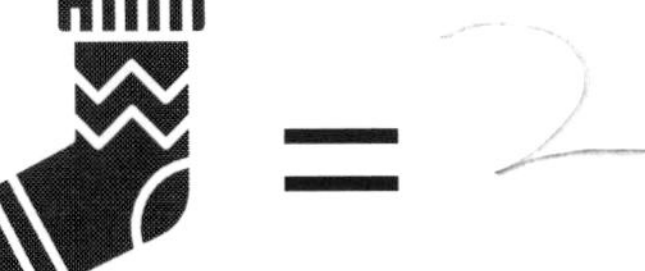 2

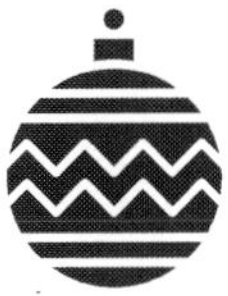

7 - ... - 3 = 2

6 - ... - ... = 3

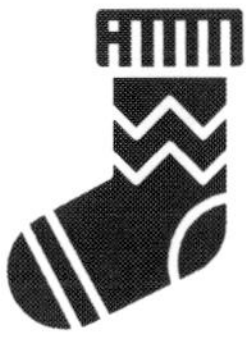

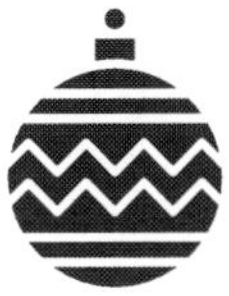

4 - ... - ... = 1

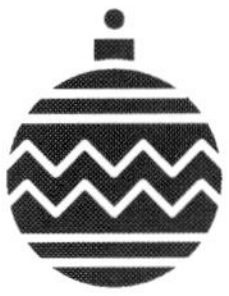

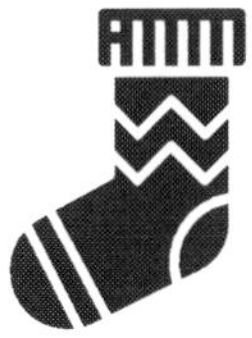

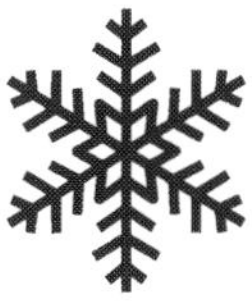

... - 1 -  = 1

USE THIS PAGE TO SHOW YOUR WORKINGS OUT

OR IF YOU DON'T NEED TO WRITE DOWN YOUR WORKINGS OUT FOR THIS ACTIVITY, USE THIS PAGE TO DRAW SOMETHING CHRISTMAS RELATED LIKE A CHRISTMAS PRESENT OR FATHER CHRISTMAS

HOW MANY ELVES? #2

THE CHRISTMAS LIST BELOW SHOWS HOW MANY ELVES ARE NEEDED TO MAKE EACH PRESENT. CAN YOU WORK OUT HOW MANY ELVES WOULD BE NEEDED FOR THE ENTIRE LIST?

ANSWER ON PAGE 54

CHRISTMAS LIST

PRESENT:	ELVES NEEDED:
TOY CAR	4
HEADPHONES	2
RUBIK'S CUBE	2
GAMES CONSOLE	6
WATER BOTTLE	3

TOTAL NUMBER OF ELVES NEEDED: 17

USE THIS PAGE TO SHOW YOUR WORKINGS OUT

OR IF YOU DON'T NEED TO WRITE DOWN YOUR WORKINGS OUT FOR THIS ACTIVITY, USE THIS PAGE TO DRAW SOMETHING CHRISTMAS RELATED LIKE A CHRISTMAS PRESENT OR FATHER CHRISTMAS

CHRISTMAS SEQUENCES #2

CAN YOU FINISH THESE MATHS SEQUENCES AND WORK OUT WHICH NUMBERS SHOULD BE IN PLACE OF THE PRESENTS?

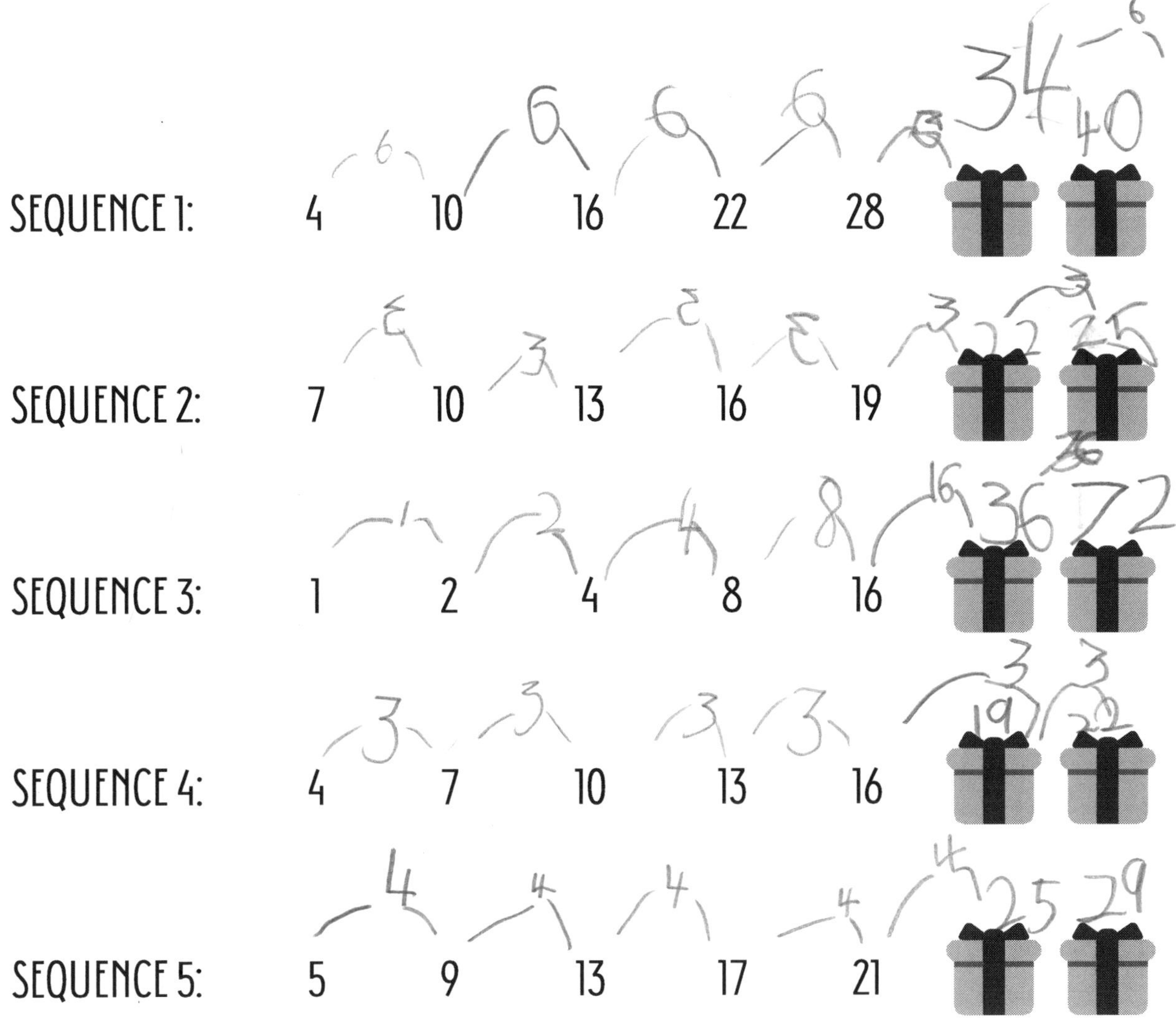

ANSWERS ON PAGE 65

USE THIS PAGE TO SHOW YOUR WORKINGS OUT

OR IF YOU DON'T NEED TO WRITE DOWN YOUR WORKINGS OUT FOR THIS ACTIVITY, USE THIS PAGE TO DRAW SOMETHING CHRISTMAS RELATED LIKE A CHRISTMAS PRESENT OR FATHER CHRISTMAS

CHRISTMAS EQUATIONS #2

CAN YOU WORK OUT HOW MUCH THE DECORATION, SNOWFLAKE AND CHRISTMAS TREE ARE WORTH?

ANSWER ON PAGE 67

 +  = 4

 +  = 6

 +  = 11

 =

 =

 =

USE THIS PAGE TO SHOW YOUR WORKINGS OUT

OR IF YOU DON'T NEED TO WRITE DOWN YOUR WORKINGS OUT FOR THIS ACTIVITY, USE THIS PAGE TO DRAW SOMETHING CHRISTMAS RELATED LIKE A CHRISTMAS PRESENT OR FATHER CHRISTMAS

12 DAYS OF CHRISTMAS #2

— SUBTRACTION —

CAN YOU COMPLETE THESE MATHS QUESTIONS BASED AROUND THE 12 DAYS OF CHRISTMAS SONG?

A) THE NUMBER OF PIPERS PIPING 11 - 2 THE NUMBER OF TURTLE DOVES = 9

B) THE NUMBER OF MAIDS-A-MILKING 8 - 6 THE NUMBER OF GEESE-A-LAYING = 2

C) THE NUMBER OF LORDS-A-LEAPING 10 - 4 THE NUMBER OF CALLING BIRDS = 6

ANSWER ON PAGE 69

1 PARTRIDGE IN A PEAR TREE	5 GOLD RINGS	9 LADIES DANCING
2 TURTLE DOVES	6 GEESE-A-LAYING	10 LORDS-A-LEAPING
3 FRENCH HENS	7 SWANS-A-SWIMMING	11 PIPERS PIPING
4 CALLING BIRDS	8 MAIDS-A-MILKING	12 DRUMMERS DRUMMING

THE ULTIMATE CHRISTMAS MATHS BOOK FOR KIDS 6-10

GREAT WORK!!

YOU'VE DONE SOME GREAT WORK SO FAR SO IT'S TIME TO TREAT YOURSELF TO A FUN ACTIVITY! COLOUR IN THE IMAGE BELOW TO BRING IT TO LIFE.

USE THIS PAGE TO SHOW YOUR WORKINGS OUT

OR IF YOU DON'T NEED TO WRITE DOWN YOUR WORKINGS OUT FOR THIS ACTIVITY, USE THIS PAGE TO DRAW SOMETHING CHRISTMAS RELATED LIKE A CHRISTMAS PRESENT OR FATHER CHRISTMAS

CHRISTMAS SUMS #3

— MORE ADDITION —

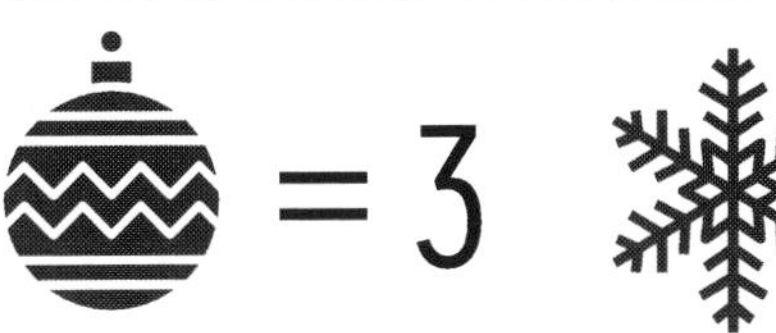 = 3 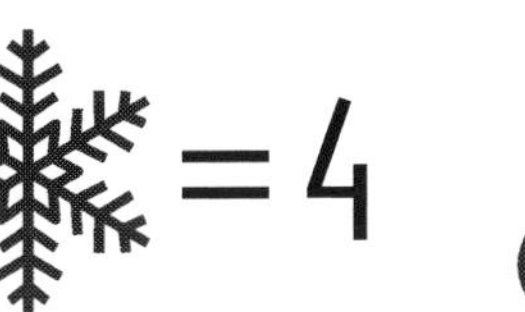 = 4  = 6

ANSWERS ON PAGE 71

\+ = 

\+ + 4 = 

\+ 2 + 3 = 11

\+ + = 

\+ 2 + = 

USE THIS PAGE TO SHOW YOUR WORKINGS OUT

OR IF YOU DON'T NEED TO WRITE DOWN YOUR WORKINGS OUT FOR THIS ACTIVITY, USE THIS PAGE TO DRAW SOMETHING CHRISTMAS RELATED LIKE A CHRISTMAS PRESENT OR FATHER CHRISTMAS

HOW MANY ELVES? #3

THE CHRISTMAS LIST BELOW SHOWS HOW MANY ELVES ARE NEEDED TO MAKE EACH PRESENT. CAN YOU WORK OUT HOW MANY ELVES WOULD BE NEEDED FOR THE ENTIRE LIST?

ANSWER ON PAGE 55

CHRISTMAS LIST

PRESENT:	ELVES NEEDED:
TV	3
CLOTHES	6
FOOTBALL SHIRT	2
CHRISTMAS HAT	6
NOTEBOOK	1

TOTAL NUMBER OF ELVES NEEDED: ______

USE THIS PAGE TO SHOW YOUR WORKINGS OUT

OR IF YOU DON'T NEED TO WRITE DOWN YOUR WORKINGS OUT FOR THIS ACTIVITY, USE THIS PAGE TO DRAW SOMETHING CHRISTMAS RELATED LIKE A CHRISTMAS PRESENT OR FATHER CHRISTMAS

CHRISTMAS SEQUENCES #3

CAN YOU FINISH THESE MATHS SEQUENCES AND WORK OUT WHICH NUMBERS SHOULD BE IN PLACE OF THE PRESENTS?

SEQUENCE 1:	64	32	16	8	4		
SEQUENCE 2:	4	5	7	10	14		
SEQUENCE 3:	54	46	38	30	22		
SEQUENCE 4:	9	13	17	21	25		
SEQUENCE 5:	1	7	13	19	25		

ANSWERS ON PAGE 73

USE THIS PAGE TO SHOW YOUR WORKINGS OUT

OR IF YOU DON'T NEED TO WRITE DOWN YOUR WORKINGS OUT FOR THIS ACTIVITY, USE THIS PAGE TO DRAW SOMETHING CHRISTMAS RELATED LIKE A CHRISTMAS PRESENT OR FATHER CHRISTMAS

CHRISTMAS EQUATIONS #3

CAN YOU WORK OUT HOW MUCH THE DECORATION, SNOWFLAKE AND CHRISTMAS TREE ARE WORTH?

ANSWER ON PAGE 75

 +  = 7

 +  = 8

 +  = 8

 =

 =

 =

USE THIS PAGE TO SHOW YOUR WORKINGS OUT

OR IF YOU DON'T NEED TO WRITE DOWN YOUR WORKINGS OUT FOR THIS ACTIVITY, USE THIS PAGE TO DRAW SOMETHING CHRISTMAS RELATED LIKE A CHRISTMAS PRESENT OR FATHER CHRISTMAS

12 DAYS OF CHRISTMAS #3

— MULTIPLICATION —

CAN YOU COMPLETE THESE MATHS QUESTIONS BASED AROUND THE 12 DAYS OF CHRISTMAS SONG?

A) THE NUMBER OF SWANS-A-SWIMMING 7 X 3 THE NUMBER OF FRENCH HENS = 21

B) THE NUMBER OF MAIDS-A-MILKING 9 X 11 THE NUMBER OF PIPERS PIPING = 99

C) THE NUMBER OF DRUMMERS DRUMMING 12 X 9 THE NUMBER OF LADIES DANCING = 108

ANSWER ON PAGE 77

1 PARTRIDGE IN A PEAR TREE	5 GOLD RINGS	9 LADIES DANCING
2 TURTLE DOVES	6 GEESE-A-LAYING	10 LORDS-A-LEAPING
~~3 FRENCH HENS~~	~~7 SWANS-A-SWIMMING~~	11 PIPERS PIPING
4 CALLING BIRDS	~~8 MAIDS~~-A-MILKING	12 DRUMMERS DRUMMING

THE ULTIMATE CHRISTMAS MATHS BOOK FOR KIDS 6-10

GREAT WORK!!

YOU'VE DONE SOME GREAT WORK SO FAR SO IT'S TIME TO TREAT YOURSELF TO A FUN ACTIVITY! COLOUR IN THE IMAGE BELOW TO BRING IT TO LIFE.

USE THIS PAGE TO SHOW YOUR WORKINGS OUT

OR IF YOU DON'T NEED TO WRITE DOWN YOUR WORKINGS OUT FOR THIS ACTIVITY, USE THIS PAGE TO DRAW SOMETHING CHRISTMAS RELATED LIKE A CHRISTMAS PRESENT OR FATHER CHRISTMAS

CHRISTMAS SUMS #4

— MORE SUBTRACTION —

 = 4  = 8  = 1

ANSWERS ON PAGE 79

 -  = ____

8 - - 3 = ____

9 -  - = ____

12 - - = ____

- 1 -  = ____

USE THIS PAGE TO SHOW YOUR WORKINGS OUT

OR IF YOU DON'T NEED TO WRITE DOWN YOUR WORKINGS OUT FOR THIS ACTIVITY, USE THIS PAGE TO DRAW SOMETHING CHRISTMAS RELATED LIKE A CHRISTMAS PRESENT OR FATHER CHRISTMAS

HOW MANY ELVES? #4

THE CHRISTMAS LIST BELOW SHOWS HOW MANY ELVES ARE NEEDED TO MAKE EACH PRESENT. CAN YOU WORK OUT HOW MANY ELVES WOULD BE NEEDED FOR THE ENTIRE LIST?

ANSWER ON PAGE 56

CHRISTMAS LIST

PRESENT:	ELVES NEEDED:
LAPTOP	8
GUITAR	4
PHONE	3
FOOTBALL GOAL	5
SOCKS	3

TOTAL NUMBER OF ELVES NEEDED: 23

USE THIS PAGE TO SHOW YOUR WORKINGS OUT

OR IF YOU DON'T NEED TO WRITE DOWN YOUR WORKINGS OUT FOR THIS ACTIVITY, USE THIS PAGE TO DRAW SOMETHING CHRISTMAS RELATED LIKE A CHRISTMAS PRESENT OR FATHER CHRISTMAS

CHRISTMAS SEQUENCES #4

CAN YOU FINISH THESE MATHS SEQUENCES AND WORK OUT WHICH NUMBERS SHOULD BE IN PLACE OF THE PRESENTS?

SEQUENCE 1:	3	14	25	36	47		
SEQUENCE 2:	73	65	57	49	41		
SEQUENCE 3:	3	6	12	24	48		
SEQUENCE 4:	9	18	27	36	45		
SEQUENCE 5:	12	26	40	54	68		

ANSWERS ON PAGE 81

USE THIS PAGE TO SHOW YOUR WORKINGS OUT

OR IF YOU DON'T NEED TO WRITE DOWN YOUR WORKINGS OUT FOR THIS ACTIVITY, USE THIS PAGE TO DRAW SOMETHING CHRISTMAS RELATED LIKE A CHRISTMAS PRESENT OR FATHER CHRISTMAS

CHRISTMAS EQUATIONS #4

CAN YOU WORK OUT HOW MUCH THE DECORATION, SNOWFLAKE AND CHRISTMAS TREE ARE WORTH?

ANSWER ON PAGE 83

 +  = 9

 +  = 10

 +  = 14

 =

 =

 =

USE THIS PAGE TO SHOW YOUR WORKINGS OUT

OR IF YOU DON'T NEED TO WRITE DOWN YOUR WORKINGS OUT FOR THIS ACTIVITY, USE THIS PAGE TO DRAW SOMETHING CHRISTMAS RELATED LIKE A CHRISTMAS PRESENT OR FATHER CHRISTMAS

12 DAYS OF CHRISTMAS #4

— DIVISION —

CAN YOU COMPLETE THESE MATHS QUESTIONS BASED AROUND THE 12 DAYS OF CHRISTMAS SONG?

A)	THE NUMBER OF DRUMMERS DRUMMING	÷	THE NUMBER OF GEESE-A-LAYING	= 2
B)	THE NUMBER OF LADIES DANCING	÷	THE NUMBER OF FRENCH HENS	= 3
C)	THE NUMBER OF DRUMMERS DRUMMING	÷	THE NUMBER OF FRENCH HENS	= 4

ANSWER ON PAGE 85

1 PARTRIDGE IN A PEAR TREE	5 GOLD RINGS	9 LADIES DANCING
2 TURTLE DOVES	6 GEESE-A-LAYING	10 LORDS-A-LEAPING
3 FRENCH HENS	7 SWANS-A-SWIMMING	11 PIPERS PIPING
4 CALLING BIRDS	8 MAIDS-A-MILKING	12 DRUMMERS DRUMMING

THE ULTIMATE CHRISTMAS MATHS BOOK FOR KIDS 6-10

GREAT WORK!!

YOU'VE DONE SOME GREAT WORK SO FAR SO IT'S TIME TO TREAT YOURSELF TO A FUN ACTIVITY! COLOUR IN THE IMAGE BELOW TO BRING IT TO LIFE.

THE ULTIMATE CHRISTMAS MATHS BOOK FOR KIDS 6-10

ANSWERS

CHRISTMAS SUMS #1

— ADDITION —

= 4  = 2 = 1

+ = 6

+ + 4 = 9

+ 2 + 3 = 6

+ +  = 7

+ 2 +  = 5

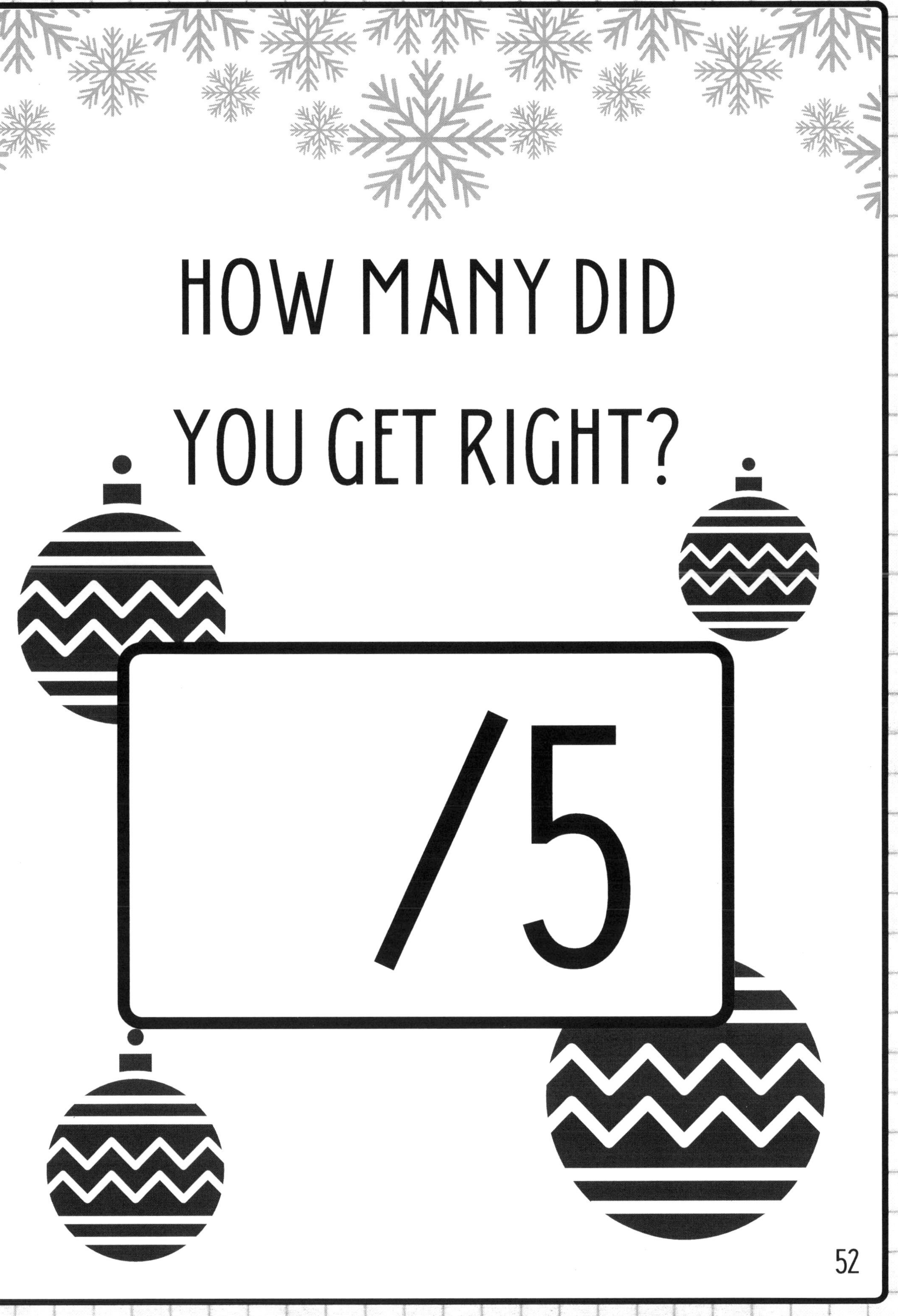
HOW MANY DID
YOU GET RIGHT?
/5

HOW MANY ELVES? #1

THE CHRISTMAS LIST BELOW SHOWS HOW MANY ELVES ARE NEEDED TO MAKE EACH PRESENT. CAN YOU WORK OUT HOW MANY ELVES WOULD BE NEEDED FOR THE ENTIRE LIST?

CHRISTMAS LIST

PRESENT:	ELVES NEEDED:
BOX OF CHOCOLATES	2
BOARD GAME	3
COMPUTER GAME	1
NEW SHOES	4
COLOURING BOOK	2

$2 + 3 + 1 + 4 + 2 = 12$

TOTAL NUMBER OF ELVES NEEDED: 12

HOW MANY ELVES? #2

THE CHRISTMAS LIST BELOW SHOWS HOW MANY ELVES ARE NEEDED TO MAKE EACH PRESENT. CAN YOU WORK OUT HOW MANY ELVES WOULD BE NEEDED FOR THE ENTIRE LIST?

CHRISTMAS LIST

PRESENT:	ELVES NEEDED:
TOY CAR	4
HEADPHONES	2
RUBIK'S CUBE	2
GAMES CONSOLE	6
WATER BOTTLE	3

4+2+2+6+3 = 17

TOTAL NUMBER OF ELVES NEEDED: 17

HOW MANY ELVES? #3

THE CHRISTMAS LIST BELOW SHOWS HOW MANY ELVES ARE NEEDED TO MAKE EACH PRESENT. CAN YOU WORK OUT HOW MANY ELVES WOULD BE NEEDED FOR THE ENTIRE LIST?

CHRISTMAS LIST

PRESENT:	ELVES NEEDED:
TV	3
CLOTHES	6
FOOTBALL SHIRT	2
CHRISTMAS HAT	6
NOTEBOOK	1

3+6+2+6+1 = 18

TOTAL NUMBER OF ELVES NEEDED: 18

HOW MANY ELVES? #4

THE CHRISTMAS LIST BELOW SHOWS HOW MANY ELVES ARE NEEDED TO MAKE EACH PRESENT. CAN YOU WORK OUT HOW MANY ELVES WOULD BE NEEDED FOR THE ENTIRE LIST?

CHRISTMAS LIST

PRESENT:	ELVES NEEDED:
LAPTOP	8
GUITAR	4
PHONE	3
FOOTBALL GOAL	5
SOCKS	3

8+4+3+5+3 = 23

TOTAL NUMBER OF ELVES NEEDED: 23

CHRISTMAS SEQUENCES #1

CAN YOU FINISH THESE MATHS SEQUENCES AND WORK OUT WHICH NUMBERS SHOULD BE IN PLACE OF THE PRESENTS?

SEQUENCE 1: 2 5 8 11 14 17 20

INCREASE PREVIOUS NUMBER BY 3

SEQUENCE 2: 1 3 5 7 9 11 13

INCREASE PREVIOUS NUMBER BY 2

SEQUENCE 3: 3 6 9 12 15 18 21

INCREASE PREVIOUS NUMBER BY 3

SEQUENCE 4: 2 6 10 14 18 22 26

INCREASE PREVIOUS NUMBER BY 4

SEQUENCE 5: 3 8 13 18 23 28 33

INCREASE PREVIOUS NUMBER BY 5

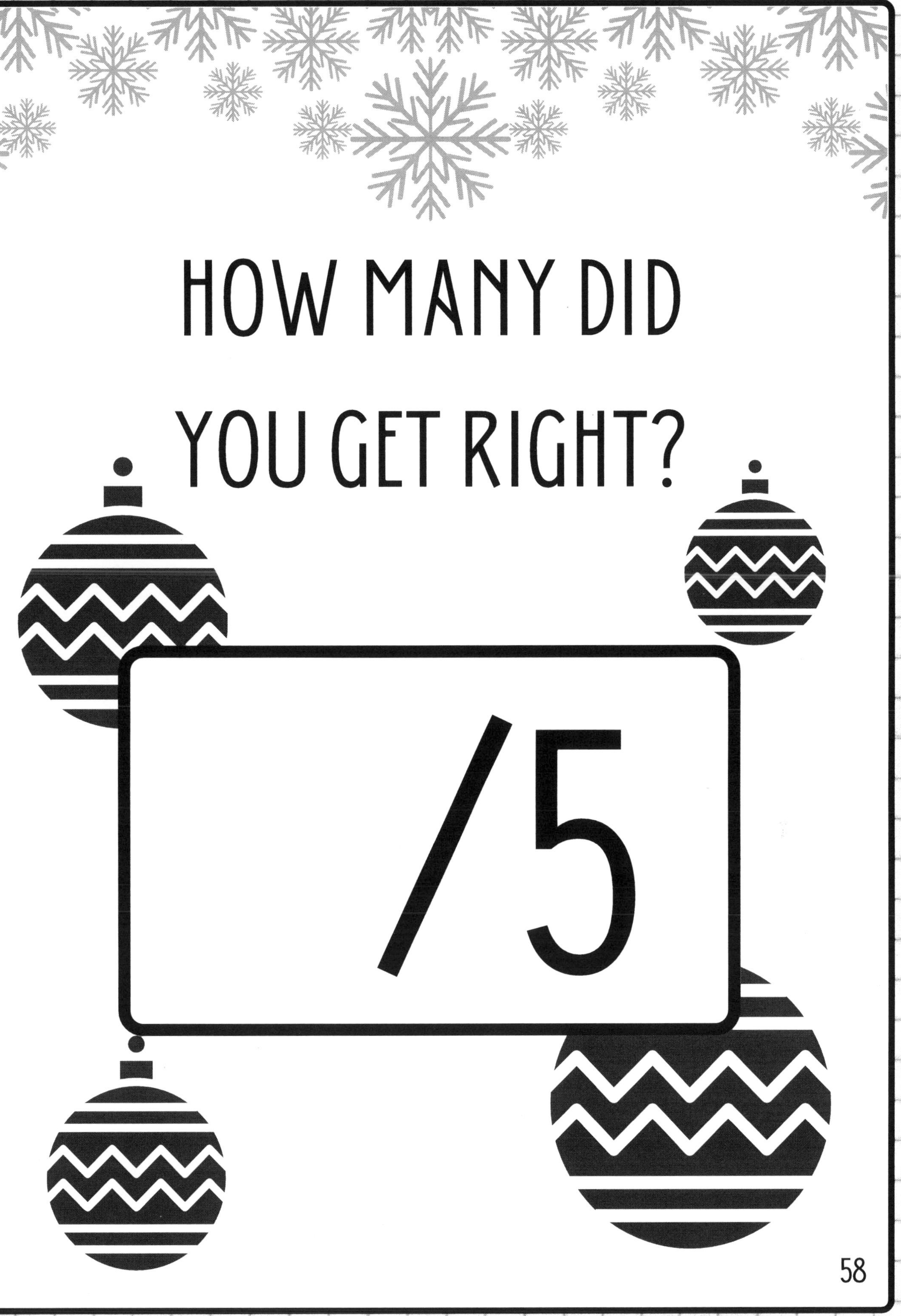

HOW MANY DID YOU GET RIGHT?

/5

CHRISTMAS EQUATIONS #1

CAN YOU WORK OUT HOW MUCH THE DECORATION, SNOWFLAKE AND CHRISTMAS TREE ARE WORTH?

 +  = 3

 +  = 7

 +  = 7

 = 3

 = 2

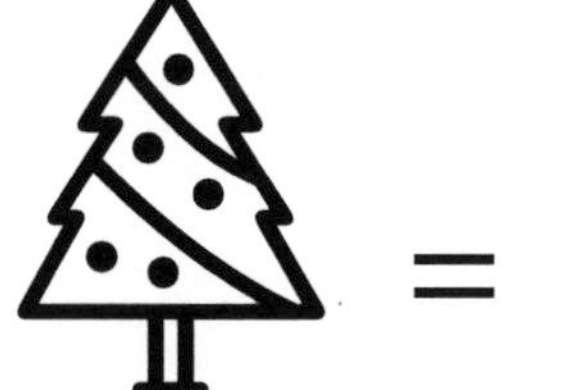 = 1

HOW MANY DID
YOU GET RIGHT?
/3

12 DAYS OF CHRISTMAS #1

— ADDITION —

CAN YOU COMPLETE THESE MATHS QUESTIONS BASED AROUND THE 12 DAYS OF CHRISTMAS SONG?

A)	THE NUMBER OF FRENCH HENS	+	THE NUMBER OF GOLD RINGS	=	8
B)	THE NUMBER OF MAIDS-A-MILKING	+	THE NUMBER OF PIPERS PIPING	=	19
C)	THE NUMBER OF DRUMMERS DRUMMING	+	THE NUMBER OF LADIES DANCING	=	21

1 PARTRIDGE IN A PEAR TREE	5 GOLD RINGS	9 LADIES DANCING
2 TURTLE DOVES	6 GEESE-A-LAYING	10 LORDS-A-LEAPING
3 FRENCH HENS	7 SWANS-A-SWIMMING	11 PIPERS PIPING
4 CALLING BIRDS	8 MAIDS-A-MILKING	12 DRUMMERS DRUMMING

HOW MANY DID YOU GET RIGHT?

/3

CHRISTMAS SUMS #2

— SUBTRACTION —

= 2   = 3    = 1

\- = 2

7 - - 3 = 2

6 - - = 3

4 - - = 1

\- 1 -  = 1

HOW MANY DID
YOU GET RIGHT?
/5

CHRISTMAS SEQUENCES #2

CAN YOU FINISH THESE MATHS SEQUENCES AND WORK OUT WHICH NUMBERS SHOULD BE IN PLACE OF THE PRESENTS?

SEQUENCE 1: 4 10 16 22 28 34 40

INCREASE PREVIOUS NUMBER BY 6

SEQUENCE 2: 7 10 13 16 19 22 25

INCREASE PREVIOUS NUMBER BY 3

SEQUENCE 3: 1 2 4 8 16 32 64

DOUBLE THE PREVIOUS NUMBER

SEQUENCE 4: 4 7 10 13 16 19 22

INCREASE PREVIOUS NUMBER BY 3

SEQUENCE 5: 5 9 13 17 21 25 29

INCREASE PREVIOUS NUMBER BY 4

HOW MANY DID
YOU GET RIGHT?
/5

CHRISTMAS EQUATIONS #2

CAN YOU WORK OUT HOW MUCH THE DECORATION, SNOWFLAKE AND CHRISTMAS TREE ARE WORTH?

 +  = 4

 +  = 6

 +  = 11

 = 4

 = 1

 = 3

HOW MANY DID
YOU GET RIGHT?
/3

12 DAYS OF CHRISTMAS #2

— SUBTRACTION —

CAN YOU COMPLETE THESE MATHS QUESTIONS BASED AROUND THE 12 DAYS OF CHRISTMAS SONG?

A)	THE NUMBER OF PIPERS PIPING	-	THE NUMBER OF TURTLE DOVES	=	9
B)	THE NUMBER OF MAIDS-A-MILKING	-	THE NUMBER OF GEESE-A-LAYING	=	2
C)	THE NUMBER OF LORDS-A-LEAPING	-	THE NUMBER OF CALLING BIRDS	=	6

1 PARTRIDGE IN A PEAR TREE	5 GOLD RINGS	9 LADIES DANCING
2 TURTLE DOVES	6 GEESE-A-LAYING	10 LORDS-A-LEAPING
3 FRENCH HENS	7 SWANS-A-SWIMMING	11 PIPERS PIPING
4 CALLING BIRDS	8 MAIDS-A-MILKING	12 DRUMMERS DRUMMING

HOW MANY DID
YOU GET RIGHT?
/3

CHRISTMAS SUMS #3

— MORE ADDITION —

= 3 = 4 = 6

+ =   7

+ + 4 =   13

+ 2 + 3 =   11

+ +  =   13

+ 2 +  =   12

HOW MANY DID
YOU GET RIGHT?
/5

CHRISTMAS SEQUENCES #3

CAN YOU FINISH THESE MATHS SEQUENCES AND WORK OUT WHICH NUMBERS SHOULD BE IN PLACE OF THE PRESENTS?

SEQUENCE 1: 64 32 16 8 4 2 1

HALF THE PREVIOUS NUMBER

SEQUENCE 2: 4 5 7 10 14 19 25

ADD 1 MORE THAN THE PREVIOUS AMOUNT ADDED

SEQUENCE 3: 54 46 38 30 22 14 6

DECREASE PREVIOUS NUMBER BY 8

SEQUENCE 4: 9 13 17 21 25 29 33

INCREASE PREVIOUS NUMBER BY 4

SEQUENCE 5: 1 7 13 19 25 31 37

INCREASE PREVIOUS NUMBER BY 6

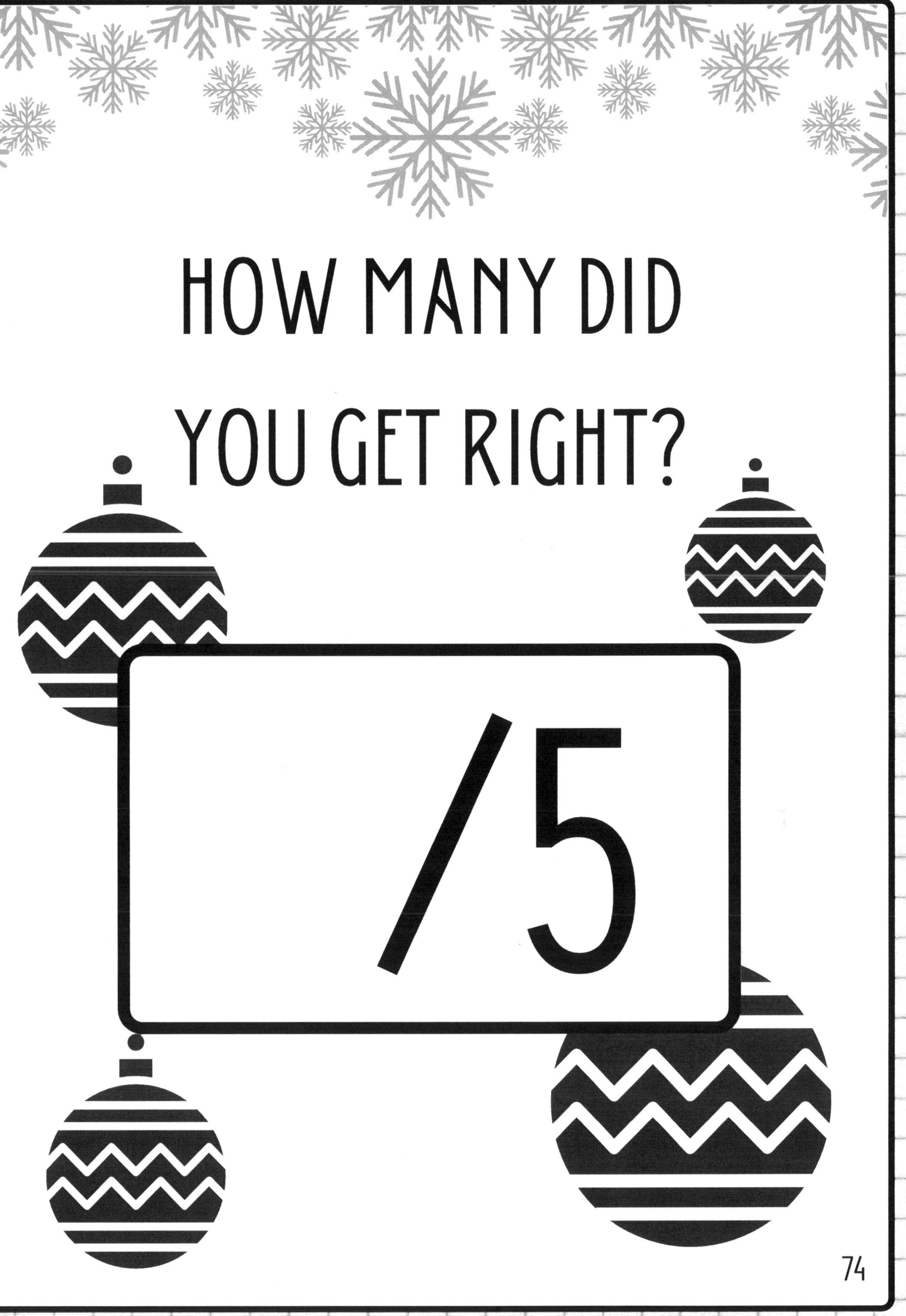
HOW MANY DID
YOU GET RIGHT?
/5

CHRISTMAS EQUATIONS #3

CAN YOU WORK OUT HOW MUCH THE DECORATION, SNOWFLAKE AND CHRISTMAS TREE ARE WORTH?

 +  = 7

 +  = 8

 +  = 8

 = 2

 = 3

 = 4

HOW MANY DID
YOU GET RIGHT?
/3

12 DAYS OF CHRISTMAS #3

— MULTIPLICATION —

CAN YOU COMPLETE THESE MATHS QUESTIONS BASED AROUND THE 12 DAYS OF CHRISTMAS SONG?

A)	THE NUMBER OF SWANS-A-SWIMMING	X	THE NUMBER OF FRENCH HENS	=	21
B)	THE NUMBER OF MAIDS-A-MILKING	X	THE NUMBER OF PIPERS PIPING	=	88
C)	THE NUMBER OF DRUMMERS DRUMMING	X	THE NUMBER OF LADIES DANCING	=	108

1 PARTRIDGE IN A PEAR TREE
2 TURTLE DOVES
3 FRENCH HENS
4 CALLING BIRDS
5 GOLD RINGS
6 GEESE-A-LAYING
7 SWANS-A-SWIMMING
8 MAIDS-A-MILKING
9 LADIES DANCING
10 LORDS-A-LEAPING
11 PIPERS PIPING
12 DRUMMERS DRUMMING

HOW MANY DID
YOU GET RIGHT?
/3

CHRISTMAS SUMS #4

— MORE SUBTRACTION —

= 4  = 8  = 1

 - = 7

8 - - 3 = 1

9 - - = 4

12 - - = 7

- 1 -  = 6

HOW MANY DID
YOU GET RIGHT?
/5

CHRISTMAS SEQUENCES #4

CAN YOU FINISH THESE MATHS SEQUENCES AND WORK OUT WHICH NUMBERS SHOULD BE IN PLACE OF THE PRESENTS?

SEQUENCE 1: 3 14 25 36 47 58 69

INCREASE THE PREVIOUS NUMBER BY 11

SEQUENCE 2: 73 65 57 49 41 33 25

DECREASE PREVIOUS NUMBER BY 8

SEQUENCE 3: 3 6 12 24 48 96 192

DOUBLE THE PREVIOUS NUMBER

SEQUENCE 4: 9 18 27 36 45 54 63

INCREASE PREVIOUS NUMBER BY 9

SEQUENCE 5: 12 26 40 54 68 82 96

INCREASE PREVIOUS NUMBER BY 14

HOW MANY DID YOU GET RIGHT?

/5

CHRISTMAS EQUATIONS #4

CAN YOU WORK OUT HOW MUCH THE DECORATION, SNOWFLAKE AND CHRISTMAS TREE ARE WORTH?

 +  = 9

 +  = 10

  +  = 14

 = 4

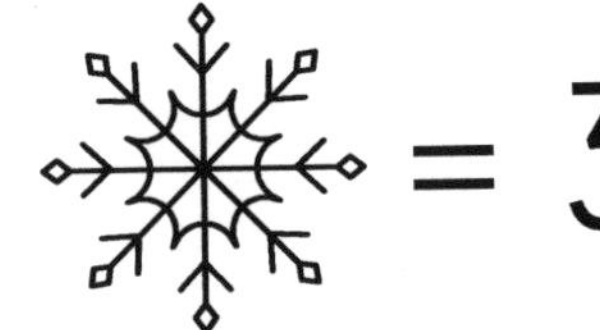 = 3

 = 6

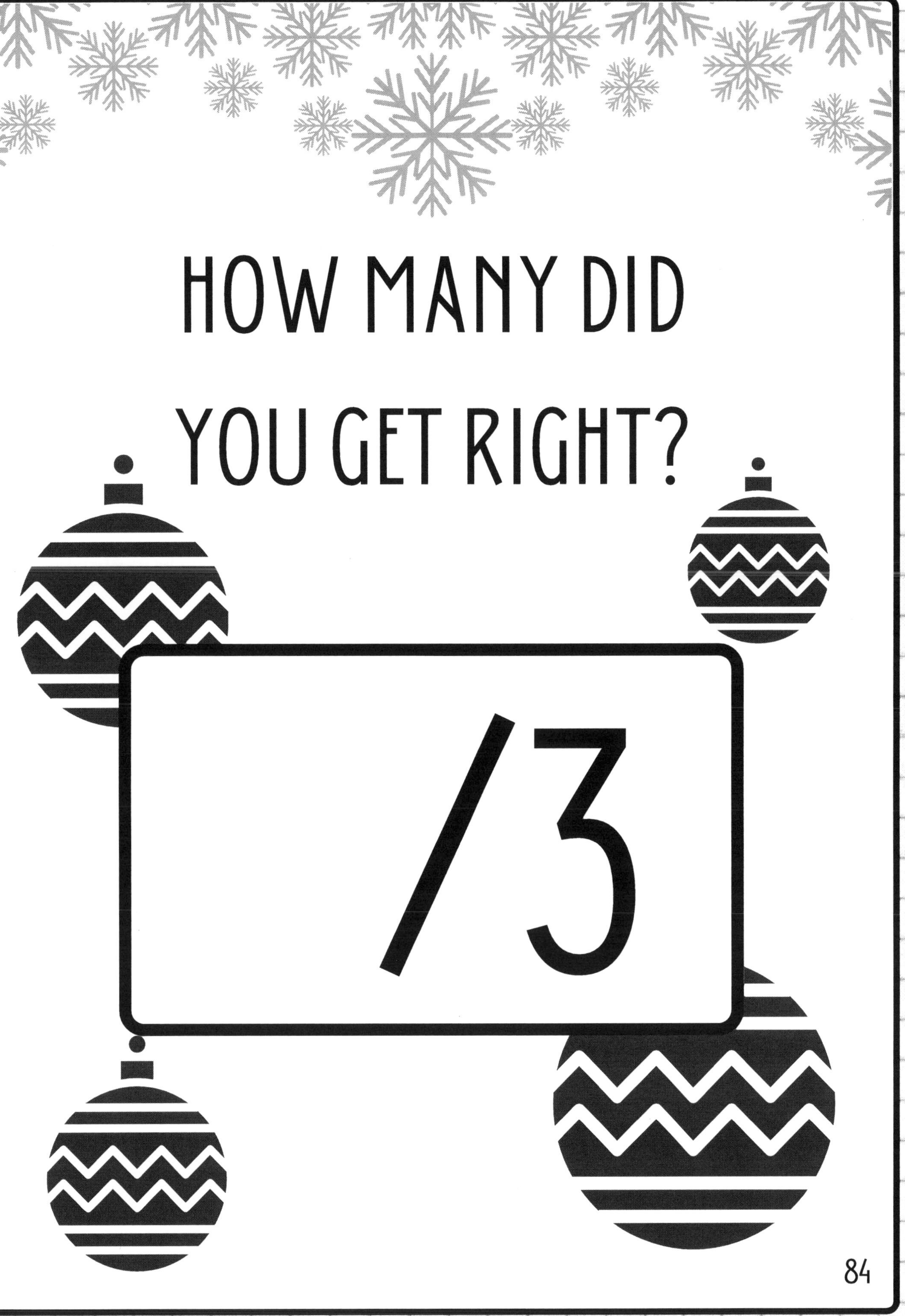
HOW MANY DID
YOU GET RIGHT?
/3

12 DAYS OF CHRISTMAS #4

— DIVISION —

CAN YOU COMPLETE THESE MATHS QUESTIONS BASED AROUND THE 12 DAYS OF CHRISTMAS SONG?

A)	THE NUMBER OF DRUMMERS DRUMMING	÷	THE NUMBER OF GEESE-A-LAYING	=	2
B)	THE NUMBER OF LADIES DANCING	÷	THE NUMBER OF FRENCH HENS	=	3
C)	THE NUMBER OF DRUMMERS DRUMMING	÷	THE NUMBER OF FRENCH HENS	=	4

1 PARTRIDGE IN A PEAR TREE	5 GOLD RINGS	9 LADIES DANCING
2 TURTLE DOVES	6 GEESE-A-LAYING	10 LORDS-A-LEAPING
3 FRENCH HENS	7 SWANS-A-SWIMMING	11 PIPERS PIPING
4 CALLING BIRDS	8 MAIDS-A-MILKING	12 DRUMMERS DRUMMING

HOW MANY DID YOU GET RIGHT?

/3

Printed in Great Britain
by Amazon